*For Debra,
with much
gratitude.*

CITY OF STARLINGS

DANIEL NATHAN TERRY

Daniel Nathan Terry

SIBLING RIVALRY PRESS
LITTLE ROCK, ARKANSAS

WWW.SIBLINGRIVALRYPRESS.COM

Sibling Rivalry Press, LLC
PO Box 26147
Little Rock, AR 72221

info@siblingrivalrypress.com

www.siblingrivalrypress.com

ISBN: 978-1-937420-86-4

Library of Congress Control Number: 2014959473

First Sibling Rivalry Press Edition, March 2015

For Andrea

III

AFTERWARDS

Fog bank's gray band hangs low over the field.
Cautious uprising; the dead are torn

between morning light and Cimmerian soil.
Visitations can't last; every prestidigitation

depends on faith, and at best, evanesces
into loss. What is this fascination with

the dead? Why conjure them into shifts
of air, into each turn in the weather?

The living push on through this stratus
with such hunger, with such thirst. Look

into this earthbound cloud and see seven ibises
needling the shorn weeds for something to sustain

them, heads and necks of sewing machines
threading the furrows, the broken blades, last season's

blooms so desiccated no one would know them
now. While the dead make their choices—whether to stay

a bit longer or make their quiet apologies—the living
must continue their own, impossible task: stitching the earth

each time sorrow or longing rips it wide.

WHAT IT MEANS TO HER

Black paws and nose to the winter grass, she doesn't look up
the way I do to see if there is anything worth remembering
about our walk. But then, for her, this walk is not one,

but many. Scents of yesterday's walk, and the day's before,
and day's before fill her nostrils as if all our days
are contained in this moment. So, as my eyes search

for things of value—noticing what can and can no longer
be seen—she breathes in the child who cycled by
an hour ago, the robins that dug in the grass this morning,

the cold rain that fell last Tuesday—but without the troubling
human losses like *an hour ago*, *this morning*, and *last Tuesday*.
She misses nothing and nothing ever ends.

THE DEER

I found the frozen carcass while walking the dogs.
At first I mistook it for an old, discarded carpet,
half rolled and hoar-frosted. So little remained:
the matted pelt, the pink spine, a few ribs, the head.

Something had picked the bones then left
the doe's remnants in the median near the wood's edge
at the end of my street. It was a bright morning, a holiday,
the cold air chalked the road white.

My dogs steamed at the ends of their leads,
eyes down, noses interrogating the path before them,
driven by the need, so natural to them, to finish
what something else had begun. But I, being human,

couldn't bear to see the dogs I nestled with at night,
the dogs that knew the words *ball, breakfast, kisses,*
even my given name, revert to what they would have been
without knowing me. So we walked on,

but the deer came with us——a staggering emptiness
behind my human eyes.

AT THE CORNER OF
SHIPYARD AND INDEPENDENCE

since Christmas, four elderly
drifters—possibly headed
farther south for the winter—
have stood at the crossroads as
human signs. Paid by the day
to advertise for the local gym,
they have brandished placards
that read *Lose Weight Now!*
Only $19.95 a month! Times are
tough. Memberships are down
all over town. And the shabby,
skinny men do draw attention.

But this morning they are
gone. I idle at the light,
waiting for the green arrow,
wondering where the men are
now—it is so cold today. Cars
turn left toward the mall and
the university, trucks pass by
in the oncoming lane headed
for the port and its towers of
metal containers filled with
imported goods waiting to be
hauled across America.

In the scrub that grows in the
corners of this intersection, a
redbird bursts into song on a
myrtle branch that's tangled
with old tinsel. And on the
gravel shoulder, a crow picks

through a scattered bag of
trash, warblers perch on
the tips of briars to warm
themselves in the sun. We are
nothing compared to these
winter birds—who find here,
of all places, what they need.

CITY OF CROWS

My coat is too thin, but I don't want walls around me.
Too cold for camellias, white flowers burn to parchment

beneath the pines. Beneath the retreating hounds
of the night, the remains of the moon still hanging

in the warm illusion of the gilding sky. I don't want to remain
in my dead garden, don't want to walk upon the frozen ground,

even in my shoes. The crows of dawn agree, are adamant; they urge
me over the fields beyond the sadness of this neighborhood.

Even the houses of the poor, they insist, are beautiful
from the winter sky. But what kind of man follows

the advice of crows? They say the earth is not eternal,
that work is useless, that this day is already someone's last.

Wander, wander, they insist. Someone has lost something needed.
Someone else has thrown away love. From the top of the city,

we will come upon these both, and these are all we require.

LUCKY

At dawn, in the middle of the street, I found a dead pup,
no more than three months old, still warm, head crushed
by a tire, mouth shattered, seeping a red silence

into the filthy blacktop. I turned my back on him,
cursed his blonde hide, crossed paws, ruined black lips
and mangled smile that couldn't grant five minutes

for me to wipe the sleep from my eyes, pour coffee,
notice him sitting up in the street, rush to rescue him
from the oncoming truck.

When I returned to bury him, I saw another face—a brother—
darker, thicker furred than his dead sibling,
curled against the cold body,

wasting his warmth on his beloved dead, but fearless
and waiting for me—to stretch from my sorrow
and lift him back into the arms of the living.

AZALEA WITH CROWS

What to make of one crow,
black and chattering to the white

dogwood flowers, as his mate flaps down
to earth, amid azaleas, to tug and tear

the meat from the severed wing
that once lifted one of their own. The azaleas

bloom too early this year. Warm winter,
so much sun so soon, and the buds

can't hold their tongues
a moment longer; mouths of red,

pink, and white gape in the heat;
their colors made of wind and rain

tell tales of the dead they've dredged up
from the dirt. *Listen:* one scarlet flower

releases the last caw from a crow's
moth-white skull cradled in a web

of feeder roots just below the mulch.
The living perch above it all in a tree

of white crosses. The female cleans her beak
on a branch. Azalea translates into *dry earth; ablaze,*

though, at home it is called *siangish shu,*
or *shrub that is longing for home.*

HOME

I had seen a homeless young man, heroin-lean, who walked a red-gold mongrel leashed with a nylon cord enter and exit the woods each day. I knew he was living in the tangle of turkey oaks and reindeer moss.

When I walked my own dogs past the woods I wondered how he fed his dog. Did the dog fend for itself? Did it get his leftovers or did it get the lion's share while the young man needled the vein in his slender arm?

And so I led my dogs to the woods, walked through the tangles, telling myself I was there to help, but driven by something unnamable. Signs of men were everywhere: empty beer cans, dirty clothes, used condoms. Two, faded orange Trick-or-Treat pails shaped like Jack-O-Lanterns hung from a bare branch to collect rainwater.

Finally we came upon a clearing and in the clearing was a room without walls—a filthy, mildewed sofa, two stained, ripped easy chairs, a coffee table, a tattered rug streaked with mold and dusted in frost. The dogs sniffed the rug, pulled forward. I released them. They circled twice around the rug, then lay down as if we had come home.

CITY OF STARLINGS
Wilmington, NC

Cold spell in July and the lake gives in
and gives up the black secrets of snakebirds and the ridiculous

white of egrets. I walk the banks of Greenfield Lake as it lies
in the center of the old town, last pseudo-natural

space enclosed by pseudo-urbanity. Read: Southern City. Colonized:
azaleas from China, camellias from Japan,

the exotics of the Fragrance Garden plaqued with a quote
from Millay, "I know not how such things can be."

And neither do I. How can this ancient slash of brack
and slime, of cypress and swamp rose, exist

so imprisoned by the red, pink, and flesh-
white hybridized buds of *azalea indica* that will spill

their pasts, in April, like the innards of something
butchered? Or like the blood and bone of the black men

and women slaughtered here in what most locals still call
the Insurrection of 1898. Should I be shaken

by the past of a town that protests its innocence
with every season? Azalea Belles, the lovely young women

of New Hanover, black and white, paraded each spring
in hoopskirted organdy and lace, in the finery of daughters

and wives of slave-owners. Meanwhile, the mockingbird
plays back the midnight call of the whip-poor-will,

as invisible as the original singer was last night.
Meanwhile, a flock of European starlings,

black feathers tin-punched with arrowheads of false-light,
torment the sky, smoke storm of wings. Do they dream

of exodus? Would they traverse the sea,
if their short pinions could carry them

home? Is it instinct or rage that drives them
to rip the naked young bluebirds from the hollows

of trees? Should I be surprised when we, who must live here,
turn against each other? So much of what I love in this place

never wanted to be here. Beneath a myrtle
choked with Spanish moss, a golden cassia blooms.

Overhead, the starlings now twist and bronze the failing daylight.
Their song is otherworldly and constant: a high,

cascading warble somewhere between violin
and the cry of a garden gate, rusted, swinging shut

upon your leaving. A song unlike any other. It is the song
that iron would sing if it had a heart. More beautiful than ever,

this horrible town.

TAMA-NO-URA

camellia japonica

In English its name is *the hidden jewel*. Found
in 1947 by a poor woodsman in a forest near Nagasaki,
not so far from where the bomb fell
and not so long after, it is the only wild japonica
that is red, edged in white. Adding to its beauty,
its growth is vigorous, though its habit is weeping.

To see it, imagine a flower of red fire giving off white smoke.
Or a duster of cerise feathers edged in chalk,
meant only for small hands. Imagine a cloisonné cup
of red enamel and mother of pearl—something given
by someone believed to be lost, something precious,
if only to you, now returned. Imagine a beautiful bell
of silence.

JITSU-GETSU-SEI
(THE SUN, THE MOON, THE STARS)
camellia japonica var. 'Higo'

Favored by Samurai who believed
as much in the cultivation of beauty
as in the art of war,

the Higo has never caught on in America.
The center of its flower is a sunburst
of hundreds of golden stamens, perfectly formed.

But the single petals are small and misshapen.
Rather than shun the flowers for their flaw,
the Samurai saw the distorted petals as a reinforcement

of the perfection in the flower's heart.
Hundreds of years before I planted Jitsu-getsu-sei
in my garden, they wrote poems to its ancestors

and planted rootings of these Higos
by the graves of friends and lovers.
It is one of the few camellias that drops its aging flowers

cleanly from the branch onto the earth,
each fallen blossom like a spirit's face looking back
at its body, but without any unsightly clinging

to what has already passed.

HOME AT LUNCH

In this neighborhood of shacks
and old trailers, homeless gather
at the Stop and Shop to bum
smokes and slugs of warm tequila
from the prostitutes who work the woods
behind the shipyard, and to get the best pick
of the free bread handed out by the ministry
next door. A few dogs roam the sidewalk
that flanks the local TV station,
where, just this moment, the midday anchor tells
the camera that a former winner of *American Idol*
will perform at April's Azalea Festival.
It is February. In the front yard
of the condemned house across the street,
a lone camellia, disastrously beautiful, blooms
in three distinct shades of red.

FERAL

Three golden dogs sprawled
in the dawn cold, honeyed

bellies full of secrets as they lie
behind the illusion

of a low picket of ruby glass,
the sun behind it, trick of the light

keeping reality at bay.
Then the truth of shadows:

outlines revealing upturned ribs
in the bloodied stubble

of corn half-rising from the furrows
beside the white, clapboard church.

Even in sleep, this feral pack
guards the bones of the doe

they ravaged. Let go
of what you believed

you saw. Now, your eyes are full
of beauty and loss. What more

could you pray to see?

8 MINUTES

It happened this way——while my friend
was asking her husband to hang a white sheet
over the kitchen door so no one could see her
and she would not have to witness the morning

light, while my friend's mother was trying
to reach me on my phone as it recharged
in the car's cigarette lighter, while my friend's
father was thinking how perfectly shaped

his stillborn granddaughter's lips were——
I was on the way to the grocery store
and the median was full of butterflies and trash
and like a fool I was thinking the world couldn't be

more beautiful. Then I looked up
through the dirty windshield and noticed
far in the distance of the bright sky——two vultures
riding the updrafts, black wings V'd

like dark fingers making the sign for victory
or for peace. All alone, I laughed out loud,
said out loud to no one——*it's anybody's guess
how the day will go.* But just then

a snowy egret flew across the rising sun——
below the vultures, above the trash
and butterflies—and for a moment the light
that had traveled 93 million miles in 8 minutes

through the darkness and emptiness of space
struck the white feathers of the passing
egret's wings, and the beauty in the translucence
of its white feathers was almost unbearable.

ONLY THE JAYS

A Cooper's hawk splits the sky,
drops into a flock of songbirds foraging
for the seed in the short grass.
                              Doves erupt
in a dozen directions, sparrows flee.
Even the gold-eyed grackles with stiletto
beaks panic into the air.
                              The hawk talons
a cardinal—bull's-eye red, confused, too slow
to action—then rises into the trees, its prey
trailing like the tail of a kite.
                              Only the jays—
harsh and unlovable, wings and tails
blue and barred as prison windows—return
to confront the killer. Their screams
                              harrow the hawk,
still his bloody beak in mid-rip, drive him
from the trees into the open where the jays dive
and thrust, terrifying in their numbers,
                              in their rage.
Until the hawk rises to heights beyond
their reach, they will pursue, will defend
the cardinal's corpse, will not relent—
                              as if the dead
were one of their own. The sky is medieval
with frescoed angels—lovely,
but for all their grieving, vanishing.

THIS DAY NEEDS PETER FALK

even more than *Wings of Desire* needed him—
to make sense of pain, to offer
a smoke and a cup of coffee, a moment
of real conversation. Otherwise

it's going to be another day spent walking
across this broken land—its whitewashed barriers,
its many languages. Another day beneath
this unbreakable sky—its untouchable ceiling

of marble. Another day surrounded
by the sorrowful children of murderers
burdened by the crimes of their fathers,
haunted by the flickering smiles

of the dead—who would forgive them. Or worse,
it will be another day that an angel, weary
in a threadbare coat, falls
for a depressed trapeze artist

who is unwilling to climb the rope again,
to swing above the seated children,
to deceive them with her white arms
like wings, her smile, her red hair—knowing

that by sunrise the circus will fold its tent
and the baby elephant will be led away.
I cannot bear another day this untranslatable.

THERE IS NO WAY

There is no way to un-see the dead
doe, her body stretched out below

the split rail fence of the long-abandoned,
gas station along the highway. She is beautiful

in the way empty buildings caught in the right light
can be. Beautiful with dandelions gone to seed

between her folded, unbroken forelegs.
Beautiful, the cold sun rising, bright and bloodless

behind each white gone-flower. For a moment,
before the wind rises, grace returns

to all fragile halos. There is no way to see
these clouds of light and not see the pillow

you once slept on beside me; each night
its down receiving your wishes and dreads,

each small vane and rachis billowing in the cotton sheath
taking you in like black ink into paper as it lies

beneath the pen.

THE EGRET OF GREENFIELD LAKE

There is no other stillness.
Only this slim white body.

frozen above the black
water. The trees do not know it. Nor

the stones of the path that are still
only because they have no other

choice. Nor the dead who could choose
stillness, but refuse it more often

than the living. Nothing knows this
stillness, except for this lone egret

who now, suddenly in flight, remains
the memory of stillness. And my small soul

that needs to be still even for a breath
is instead pulled up and out of me

with each beat of white wings.

THE ISLAND

It's no longer there—the small island
that swelled from the belly
of the winnowing lake during last summer's drought.

I know the winter rains have submerged it
back into the dark, but I remember how this brow of mud
served as a resting place for the black cormorants

that flew beneath the water's skin in search of sunfish,
before returning to the island to dry their open wings
like children's bathing suits hung on a clothesline.

Now, the cormorants must take their rest on the lake's surface,
breasts to the cold water, wings open like the raised sails
of small fishing boats in silhouette. I wonder—

when they dive deep into the lake, wings propelling them like fins
through veils of pond weed—if their shadows ever pass above
the submerged island, and do they remember when the island's face

pressed against the sky?

CYCLING THROUGH THE GRAVEYARD

Old woman in the open car, parked far
enough from the graveside to sit apart
from the mourners but not so far away
not to be counted among them.
                              I want to believe
she has come to make her silent peace, to wish
well one she loved in secret, one whose parting
has long grieved her but never so much
as this new form of going away.
                              I want to believe
I understand her when she turns and looks at me
as I pass. I want to believe she knows that
I grieve too. But I do not know her
and what I want her to be as I ride by the cemetery
is just that—what I want.
                              No different really than the flock
of winter robins I have cycled through each morning
for a week: My presence first makes them skitter
ahead of me on the cold, dry grass, then my closeness
prompts their flight. For a moment I am flying
with them. We are a flock.
                              For a moment I am
one of them and I feel everything and don't think
about anything else at all. Later, I believe
they have always been with me—these robins—
with me since I was a child and chased
them across green lawns and into the sky
where I could not follow.
                              But I know these robins
cannot be the robins of my youth. I know their lives are short.
But I want to believe they are the same
birds I have always known; I want to believe
that for a moment I am one of them even though

I know better.

        But maybe I am wrong
about what I know, what I am right to believe,
in which case, I should turn this bike around
and go back to the graveyard and sit with her
for a moment and hold her hand in mine
                like *I know*.

TERRAPENE CAROLINA CAROLINA

Each May, they come from the black
lake. Slow shuffle of old women,
these mother turtles stroke

through the clipped grass, moss
covered backs like heavy green stones
floating on green water. Each year,

they crawl on their bellies,
swollen with eggs, across the footpath,
across the well-traveled road. Some

mornings, I see pairs of crows inked
against the curb, purring and clicking
as they beak and throat

the pink flesh of a mother
whose shell cracked open
like ripe fruit. This morning,

one mother has nearly finished
her great task—head lifted
to the pines above, paddle feet

rowing the sand and needles
over her children, guarding them
until emergence, and they must

make the journey to the lake.
A pair of crows watch from the pine.
One flaps its wings, but remains silent.

I, too, will return when the lizard tongues
have dropped and the pickerel weed
is silent. I will hope to see the dark coins

of her children skip in their own slow time
across the road and into the water, safe
from the memory of crows

and the ignorance of machines.
But for now, I will admire her effort,
and turn back to the lake's edge

where one swamp rose stretches
from the knees of a cypress,
close enough to the bank for me

to inhale its perfume for the first time.

GRANDFATHER

When I was twelve, you said fags
should be lined up and shot. Grandmother shook

her head and left the room. How many people,
during the evening news, had you sent

blindfolded to the wall in your mind for forgivable
crimes? Feminists, Communists, Catholics, Blacks. Everyone

who wasn't like you, sickened you. Gays were just the latest
to parade across the TV screen as painted ducks in a carnival

arcade. But I took you at your word. I had no other choice—
there was the way you kept me in your sight if I moved left

instead of right, there was the way you shouted me back in line,
and there was your WWII carbine above the mantle

that dropped a buck and made his doe burst through the thicket
and run, maddened by fear, headlong into thorns.

ELEGY FOR A MARRIAGE

for my grandparents

I

Each morning the hen crows
like a rooster, plays the role

of harbinger and husband,
filling in the gaps with a primal cry,

half-warning, half-lamentation.
She cocks her yellow eye

to heaven. Her look interrogates
the clouds, forces the revelation

of a broad-winged hawk.
It circles twice, rides the updrafts

into some other's last morning.

II

Your wife cannot walk on her own
now. Lies there day after day.

Her eyes still accuse you for being
the man you were, still shout,

but when she tries to speak,
she mews like a brambled wren.

The arms that gathered eggs,
that held you, sometimes,

at bay are X'd on her chest.
So the couch seems already

her coffin, or it would
if her fingers

weren't in constant motion.
Though empty, they worry

each other as if something
is between them.

III

The rainbowed bantam,
jungle-sleek,

with the checkered nape
of a Dominique,

secrets her infertile eggs
in the weedy thicket

far from the rotting coop
that's become

a skull—black socket-windows
and an open maw.

IV

The deep woods you loved
have been sold, logged, stripped,

the forest floor ravaged
to pay doctors who can do nothing

but prolong pain.
Even the century oaks

just past the gate—where she sat
those after-the-fight-afternoons,

naming the birds in whispers—
are gone, proving that despite your memory,

they were never yours.
Eventually everything is lost,

winnowed away,
stolen in one stroke, unless wisely

surrendered.

V

Spring storm and the roar
of the creek. In darkness

a lady's slipper is swept
from the bank into the knotted roots

of a river oak, miles away.
Furrows flood. A vole quits

his muddy burrow, scrambles
into the tangled shelter of last year's

squash and cucumber vines, nestles down
in blackness, inhales the first green

threads of life just breaking ground.
Your neglect, to him, more useful

than your best effort.

VI

Today she drums her breast
like a warrior, then

settles back upon her nest
among the weeds that give up

the laboring breath of Confederate
violets, as she anticipates

tiny earthquakes, fractures
in the alabaster shells—

life beaking its way back
to the farm. She watches you

stand at the edge of the field,
the tin bucket of dinner scraps

growing heavy in your hand.

VII

Beneath the oak's ghost—
a sapling maple.

Sixty-eight years of marriage
in the Appalachian hollows decay,

as she lies wordless, dying, ferns
uncurl from the rotting logs.

A rooster from an adjacent farm
finds his way into the valley

and crows from the returning ironwoods.
The hen turns her eggs.

Sweetbriar stretches from the shadows
and hooks onto the wounds of light

the felled trees have opened in the canopy. Blood
trilliums beat again in the undergrowth.

Against your will,
life comes down

the hill, through the shattered
forest—scattering beauty.

Relentless.

Unforgiving.

THE BOY AND THE MOTH

Blue night and the hammer of the sphinx
moth's wings as it chisels through heavy air,

as it tunnels up and into the throat
of the spine-white bloom of the angel's

trumpet. Or is this upward thrust
and percussion of need closer to the snap

shuffle of a deck of cards, hands of a gambler
who is finally winning?

It is the remembered rhythmic flick of the red jack
of hearts clipped to the spoke

of a bike ridden by a boy who is ready to go
farther than ever before, the dark man's house

only a few hundred more pumps of thigh and bone
away, now. Whatever I've done, whatever I'll do,

though some find it beautiful and some will recoil,
I've always done what I had to do.

HOW CAN I NOT BE CONCERNED

with the overgrown gardens
of ruined and empty houses,
old dogs

and the openness of their hearts,
the ghosts
who tend to them both,

art that is as concerned with beauty
as it is with its absence,
all manner of birds—pale and dark roses

climbing through the rusty diamonds
of a chain-link fence,
this world

and the next, abandoned tobacco fields
overrun with the violet tribes
of henbit

and of the golden dusters of the dead
broom sedge as they continue to sweep
the invisible air clean of now?

CYCLING TO THE SEA, YOU REALIZE

most of it exists without you—
the green loom of the saw grass marsh,

the warp and weft of the dark bayous,
the oyster beds' gray skeins. Little of it needs

you—not the harried, scuttling ghost
crab, nor the egret embroidering its light

onto the brackish water while you, pedaling
by, have just the time to pull this thread

of memory. Much of it doesn't want you
here—the heavy sky that drapes your back,

the smothering tide of salt-vapor, the needling
flies, the motorist who nearly clips you

as he flips you off and passes.
The road, he spits, *doesn't belong*

to you. And most of it, like so much else,
does not. But here, beneath you, the tarmac

receives the black stitch of your narrow tires.
And here, just ahead of you, your shadow—

a blue web of spokes and limbs—spins
out of your body and weaves into the immediate,

which, you know, would be less without you.

MAKE THE LAND

The wind rises from the earth
the way an island rises from the sea,

and so we abandon our broken boats,
and so all day we climb the mountain of the wind,

bare feet scaling its transparent cliffs,
thighs burning, trudging up

the relentless invisible. With no other way
home, what choice do we have?

SINCE I MARRIED THE PAINTER,

I've wanted to tell him
about a field of weeds and wildflowers

I pass each morning off Randall Road.
It's maddening, this swath of beauty

sandwiched between strip malls,
in the fall, at first light

before the dew burns off—
ragged tufts of goldenrod and ironweed

netted in a web of silver
against a cold blue sky.

More than once it called out
while I was lighting a smoke or switching tunes

at 50 miles an hour. More than once
I almost swerved into it

in what would have looked like suicide
or heart-failure at the wheel.

Sometimes I hear the weeds
singing through the car window.

It's a symphony of passing,
a lyricless requiem—they know

the end is near, the bulldozers will come.
They want to tell their story,

which is something close to: *We are too beautiful
for you to comprehend.* I've photographed the field

in every kind of light, written, rewritten
and trashed ten drafts, tried and failed

to share this wonder so many times I can't
stomach one more flop. It is

nearly October. So I beg the painter
to take up his paints and canvas, to come

with me. It might be the last September
I hear the field sing. Language has let me down,

and I want to remember life the way it is.

BECAUSE YOU READ ON THE WEB

that the medusa of *Turritopsis nutricula* is an immortal
jellyfish—a tiny god no more than five millimeters long
and able to bypass death, to return from its adulthood
to its childhood after breeding or suffering
some other trauma—
                    you wonder if the eternal-life
that religions promise should be reserved for these little ghosts
with their red crosses of blood lodged in transparent bodies
that float above ninety arms so thin they are nearly invisible
to the human eye, but no less the arms of a hunter.
                                    And you
               wonder,
like a philosopher twirling five millimeters of an immortal stone
between his finger and thumb, if it would be a blessing to revert
back to your own childhood, to skip the coming losses of old age,
the winnowing of strength and love that is, as a human,
unavoidable.
               And it is too simple to say that the part of you
who wants to die is the one who lights up a smoke, the one who
once
had sex with strangers in strange bedrooms and against the filthy
back walls of bars. That years ago aimed his truck at the white
trunk
of a giant, winter sycamore, floored the gas pedal
and took his hands off the wheel
                      thy will be done.
                          And it's too
                 simple
to say that the one who, this morning, envies the immortal medusa
is the one who is grateful that the truck lost traction and wheeled
safely into a hood-high snow-bank.
                 And it is wrong to say

that the one who would live forever is the one driving down
Independence Boulevard, hypnotized by the flowers of the flesh-
pink apricot trees as they drift into the black water of the roadside
ditch—each petal a half-shell that is also, before it sinks empty
into the mud, a fragile boat that could carry only the smallest of creatures,
if it were willing,

        to the safety of the other shore.

UNLIKE DOGS,

after we've been weaned, we attempt to love the world
in stages, and so we touch, and so

we kiss, yes. And, yes, eventually we open
our mouths to other tongues and we take

each other's roses with all their perfume,
thorns and decay, and transparent spit and dew

inside, beyond the white fence of our teeth
and tender garden of our palette, deep into the word—

the womb of the throat. But this, only after
we have reached out with tentative fingers

for a sleeve, a cuff, the rough skin on the back
of a hand we hope is stronger than ours. This only

after we have held it, at least for a moment—
but often hours, days—at arm's length.

Humans are so fearful of taking the world
into their mouths—the nights of black moths and blacker

moons, the swollen bud and urgent blood of the surging
oak, the light and all it obscures from our limited sight.

Danger. Everywhere. But nothing so frightening
as our need for some other from outside of our skin

to make it less painful to live within it. We need so much,
but come to it so slowly, examine and consider, weigh

in our hands, and judge if even an inch of flesh
is worthy of the terrible act of opening

our bodies, of exposing our warm, dark
chambers within where we still hide like nightmared

children. But what can timid fingertips know
of the virtues or poisons contained in the mouth

of another? And so the dog, not of the first order, handless,
thumbless, with no way to hold on to anything—and so no need

to evolve—takes the world into his mouth. And comes
to know it—between his teeth,

comes to love or hate it upon his wide tongue.
And it is up to him whether he drops it into the dirt

and moves on, or gnaws it a while, strips it
of its skins and barriers, crushes it

lovingly in his thick-boned jaw, then opens wide
his maw, lets the wider world become another holy cell

of his own beloved body.

NIGHTHAWKS

Nighthawks boomerang through the haloes
of streetlamps, skimming so close to the blacktop
a leaping child could catch one by its narrow wings

and hurl it back into the blackness. From the front steps,
the young man watches them dive in and out of the night,
beaks wide, sifting insects from the humid air. A pickup

rumbles down the street. In its wake, the nighthawks lift
and scatter like long leaves, then whirlwind
back to business. A mosquito

lights on the young man's temple, its legs soft and black
as eyelashes——then the sharp bite, blood stolen,
poison deposited—his reflexive slap too slow

to accomplish anything but crushing the miracle.
A knot rises beneath his skin which he will scratch
tomorrow like regret. His taxi arrives,

its low beams thick with life. At his feet lantana thrums
with nocturnal moths gathering nectar, escaping the feeding
in the waves of electric light, but opening themselves

to the skinks and spiders that lurk in the brambles. Bar cash
and condoms tucked in his back pocket, he walks
toward the cab as nature struggles with the equation—

comings minus goings, feathers divided by proboscises,
stars multiplied by the number of open eyes——
the sum of his need hanging in the balance.

THE 8TH OF MAY: A VOW

Upon seeing a video of a man in North Carolina firing his rifle into a sign asking citizens to Vote Against NC Amendment One.

There are oaks that remember
what we would forget—the burn of the rope,
how a body takes on more weight
the moment it breathes its last, how
the earth below shoeless feet grows
hungry for the slaughtered. There are rooms
where paint has been rolled over
blood, where the body's salt has been
vacuumed into bags of dust, where the veneer
of a nightstand still bears the imprint
of a living hand's last message. Ghosts
of children and men and women hang
from fences, linger in the corners
of dorm rooms, of courtrooms, of churches.
This is how we deal with it around here, he said,
after emptying his gun into a plea for equality, and some people
were shocked by his quivering pride. I will try
not to think of him when I stand in a room
in DC and vow to continue to love the man
I have loved for 16 years. I will try not to remember
that 17 years ago, a friend of mine opened his door
to a cry for help from the other side, only to be robbed
then stabbed to death with his own kitchen knives
because the thief felt threatened that my friend—
while begging for his life—revealed that he was gay.
I will even try not to think of my grandfather
who cannot forgive me for loving the man
who held me steady as I purchased the dress my grandmother
was to be buried in. I will try not to think of the memory
of these oaks, of those fences, of some rooms. I will say *I will*
and mean *carry on loving you until death*. I will

think of the dorm room where we first made love,
I will think of the fence around our house
and its roses that change color in the heat. I will
think of the Carolina oak that might remember
the night we kissed in the first bands of rain
from a hurricane just making landfall.

THE MEETING

All the day long, there was nothing of note.
Between classes, I sat and waited on the bench
beside the retention pond on campus.

Three duck decoys, placed there
months ago by Environmental Studies
to attract real ducks, listed in the wind—moving,

but fooling no one. I imagined how beautiful
the arrival of living mallards or teal would be—
whir of wings, the wake and ripples

they would make on the surface. But students passed
without looking. There was nothing for any of us
on the dark water. Then, just as I considered

looking for a new spot, a blue heron stretched
his slender neck from the tall, dry reeds
that lined the bank, only feet away from where I sat.

With one silver eye, wide as the winter moon,
he looked at me, as if I were the one
who was unexpected.

A STUDENT SAYS
SHE HATES NATURE POETRY

and is glad Robert Frost is dead
along with his ovenbirds and golden leaves.

She wants the poetry of pavement,
bars, dirty sheets, and drugs. Real life,

she insists, has nothing to do with birds,
forest paths, or things that grow. Never mind

her pavement's made of earth, her bar
of wood, her dirty sheets made of cotton

and the skin of the night. Never mind
that her drugs were distilled from green leaves

that were, for a moment, golden
on a mountainside that faced

the Colombian sun. Never mind that
when she takes that gold into her blood

she becomes its sister, and this reunion fills her
with something close to birdsong.

AUTUMNAL EQUINOX

Shadows stretch further, even
the short grass is the dark puzzle

box of the woods down the road.
Crows gather earlier each morning.

Soon, they will sleep in my ear,
black pinions curled in quiet,

anvil beaks to the pink canal. Soon,
they will be the first to wake me,

and when I stand, back turned
to sunrise, my shadow—a giant

capable of anything—doesn't quite
resemble me. What am I

becoming?

YOU MUST MAKE YOURSELF SMALL

and to become small
        you must lie
on your belly
        in the short grass

beside the garden,
        chin pressed into earth.
You must become
        the beetle

to see the world
        as big as it is,
to witness forests
        of fescue, each blade

a tower, to understand
        that the rose
is not yours, but a fortress
        of its own will.

DIRECTIONS TO MY PLACE
FROM WHERE YOU ARE

Take nothing that isn't vital. Dust the insides
of your shoes with music and dirt
from your hometown so you'll feel buoyed and grounded
all at once. Leave your house, your family, your youth.
Take the interstate south and drive all night. Be okay
with the fact that headlights make the road ahead of you
brighter, while your taillights are tired red eyes
telling those behind you that you are going away,
going away.
             Near dawn, take the first exit
and head into my town. Drive past welcome
signs, car dealerships. Drive past the Target
and the trees in the slash of woods down the road
that suddenly give up a night's weight of black wings——
these crows that scatter across the windshield
like seeds blown from black wishes.
                              Ignore the signs
that could lead you to another highway and away
from this place. Believe it or not, you're almost
where you're meant to be. Go past the dead
dog in the median and the crazy old
woman in the filthy skirt and Coors t-shirt
pointing a sunburned finger and swearing to the sky, or
to Jesus. Feel for them both, but don't dare think
burying anything lost or throwing the few wrinkled dollars
folded in your wallet at suffering will do any good.
                                   Don't veer
onto 21st Street, even if the car pulls that way—
there's a house down there—that in the future—
will hold more sorrow than you can imagine, more pain
than you can ease. And the woman who will live there
will have just lost her only child and will need time and
white sheets and pillowcases tacked to the inside

of the windowpanes like a bandage over the light
so the impossible wound can heal in darkness.

                        Come into the heart
of town. Slow down and circle the concrete beauty
of the fountain with its invulnerable children spouting cold
water into the air at the crossroads. Beauty is there for you
as much as it's there for anyone. Pass myrtles that spill
white petals onto the gray road like tall vases left
on a stone grave in the wind. Pass the white
mansion built by slaves, the orange-clad chain-gang
picking up trash and don't pretend you understand
anything about someone else's rage. Turn
left on 3rd. Go under the bridge that rises
and crosses the dark river and then, eventually, falls
into another town—there's nothing for you there.
Keep going. Cross the tracks.

                    Pass the abandoned
projects and the silver-leafed thorn poppies
that grow and bloom—white as fine linen—
only in the poorest soil. Stop for the light; it's there
to keep you safe from being blindsided by another traveler.
Be patient. When the light changes,
drive straight through. Turn right toward the shipyard
where the plastic things we think we need arrive
in sooty trailers that are hitched to hand-waxed cabs
of 18-wheelers bound for elsewhere. When you pass the news
station on your left, please slow down,

                  the turn is coming.
Take another left onto Worth Drive. But if you're in a hurry,
use caution—children play on this street, dogs and discarded
men wander with more than you on their minds, and sometimes
there in the middle of the road, without warning, is your old
house, your old life, old wishes you'd thought would never find y
in this place, losses that trailed you like thistledown
caught in the wake of your sudden departure. Be prepared to bra
and ease around them all. And if you get lost, call me,

                    and I'll bring you hom

LILIES

They would draw no more water
through the wounds I'd made, days before,
when I trimmed their length to suit
the stoneware vase. Yesterday, they wilted
and emptied of their beauty. I tossed them
through the open door into the rain.
They scattered and fell—handless white gloves
upon the green shelf of the boxwood.
Today I open the door to find the hedge
in full flower. What the lilies would not drink
through the cuts I'd made in their stems,
they now welcome from the rain
with every thirsty cell. And so they bloom again,
open as hands waving to someone who has returned,
to someone who has been absent
far too long.

MY HUSBAND ASKS
WHAT I WANT FOR MY 44TH BIRTHDAY

Since you ask, this year I want to write
a poem of joy, without the memory or fear
of loss. To see a luna moth in flight,

to touch, with my fingertips, the white
ermine of her body, the pale green
paper of her wings, to climb the night

beside her. I want to make love to you
like I did when I was twenty-four.
To see a fox spirit safely through headlights.

To unchain the lonely dogs next door
from their drug-addicted owner, and for good
measure, to unchain their owner from his drugs.

To heal him with words, to open his eyes of glass.
And since I will be a hero, I want you
to throw me a party like no other—

to which we invite the dead. Let's see what gifts they bring.
Let's drink with them again. But before they go home
to their bright houses, light the candles

and let's pose for a group photo—
all of us, for a moment, luminous
against the shadows.

WALKING LUCKY
THROUGH YELLOW FLOWERS

I read somewhere that dogs see the world in shades of gray,
with two exceptions: yellow and blue. What must it be like
to walk down this road, leashed to the man who loves you,

cars and windblown trash ghosting past like a train
in a black and white movie, the sky above an endless
road of azure, the gray grass beneath your paws littered

with stars?

CITY OF STARLINGS

ACKNOWLEDGMENTS

Big Muddy
Directions to My Place from Where You Are
Home at Lunch

Chautauqua
Cycling to the sea, you realize
Make the Land

Cimarron Review
My Husband Asks What I Want for My 44th Birthday
Since I married the painter,

Collective Brightness
Because you read on the web

Connotation Press
Azalea with Crows
Feral

Crab Orchard Review
The Boy and the Moth
There is no way

Cutthroat
Lucky
Unlike dogs,
Walking Lucky through Yellow Flowers
What It Means to Her

Hikmet Poetry Prize
Cycling through the Graveyard
The Egret of Greenfield Lake
You Must Make Yourself Small

Jasper
How can I not be concerned

JB Records
Afterwards

New World Writing
At the corner of Shipyard and Independence

Prime Number Magazine
Jitsu-getsu-sei
Tama-no-ura

Revolution House
8 Minutes

Salt
Autumnal Equinox

Terminus
City of Crows
Elegy for a Marriage

Southern Indiana Review
Terrapene carolina carolina

The Greensboro Review
City of Starlings

The Southeast Review
Grandfather

The The Poetry
The 8th of May: A Vow

This assignment is so gay: LGBTIQ Poets on the Art of Teaching
A student says she hates nature poetry
The Meeting

Undefined
The Deer

Weber Journal
Nighthawks

I would also like to thank the following for support, faith, and inspiration: Jeffery Berg, Benjamin, Catherine, and Carl Billingsley; Bryan Borland, Camellia, Katie Chapel, Nicole Cooley, Alfred Corn, Jill Gerard, Hermione, John Hoppenthaler, Judy Jordan, Allison Joseph and Jon Tribble, Terry Kennedy, Keith Kopka, Richard Krawiec, Lucky, Ed Madden, Missy, Malena Morling, Jason Mott, Val Neiman, Seth Pennington, Christopher Phelps, Staci Schoenfeld, Kevin Simmonds, Virgil Suarez, Pam Uschuk and Bill Root, Ocean Vuong, Vallie Lynn Watson, Marcus Wicker.

And, as always, my family.

DANIEL NATHAN TERRY is the son of a Baptist Minister and a Librarian. A former landscaper and horticulturist, Daniel is the author of three other books of poetry: *Waxwings* (2012); *Capturing the Dead* (2008) which won The Stevens Prize; and a chapbook, *Days of Dark Miracles* (2011). His poems and short stories have appeared, or are forthcoming, in numerous publications, including *Cimarron Review*, *The Greensboro Review*, *Crab Orchard Review*, and *New South*. His debut novel, *The Guardian*, is forthcoming from Lethe Press. He serves on the advisory board of One Pause Poetry and assists with Spilt This Rock Poetry Festival. He lives in Wilmington, North Carolina, with his husband, painter and printmaker, Benjamin Billingsley.

Sibling Rivalry Press is an independent publishing house based in Little Rock, Arkansas. Our mission is to publish work that disturbs and enraptures.

WWW.SIBLINGRIVALRYPRESS.COM

This book was produced, in part, due to the support of the non-profit Sibling Rivalry Press Foundation. The Sibling Rivalry Press Foundation assists small presses and small press authors through grants and fiscal sponsorship.

WWW.SRPFOUNDATION.ORG

CPSIA information can be obtained
at www.ICGtesting.com
Printed in the USA
FFOW02n2125100215
10965FF